THE MENTALLY TOUGH ALPACA

A CHILDREN'S BOOK ABOUT EXPECTATIONS, LETTING GO, FULFILLMENT, AND STAYING RESILIENT

WRITTEN BY
CHARLOTTE DANE

ILLUSTRATED BY
ADAM RIONG

THE MENTALLY TOUGH ALPACA

→ WISHES →

→ EXPECTATION →

→ DESIRES →

We all have expectations in life. We think things will go a certain way. But when they don't, most of us become upset and struggle.

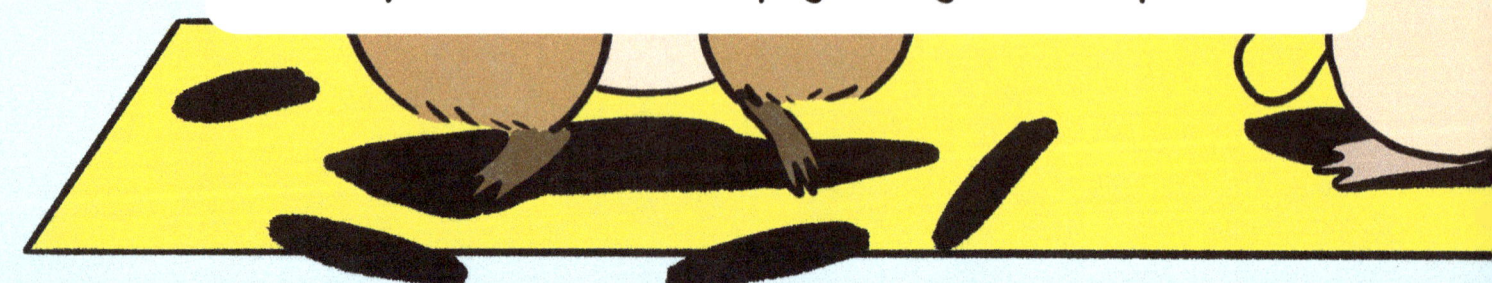

Once, Alpaca entered a juggling competition that he had practiced hard for. He wanted to win, but he ended up getting fourth place.

Alpaca was able to move on because he knew that he tried his best, and the rest was out of his control.

Another time, Alpaca and his friends were trying out to be the goalie of the soccer team. Everyone wanted it!

Alpaca was only fourth best at it, but that was fine with him. He didn't NEED to be goalie. He could play striker too!

Alpaca needed a lot of practice to even draw stick figures! He was upset at first, but realized that just because he wanted something, didn't mean it was going to happen.

Alpaca had amazing mental toughness and nothing ever bothered him too much, but he was not always like this.

Not too long ago, he would expect situations to all go a certain way. He was so focused on his expectation that if it didn't happen, he would become incredibly upset.

For example, whenever Alpaca would play basketball with his friends, he expected that he would score the most points.

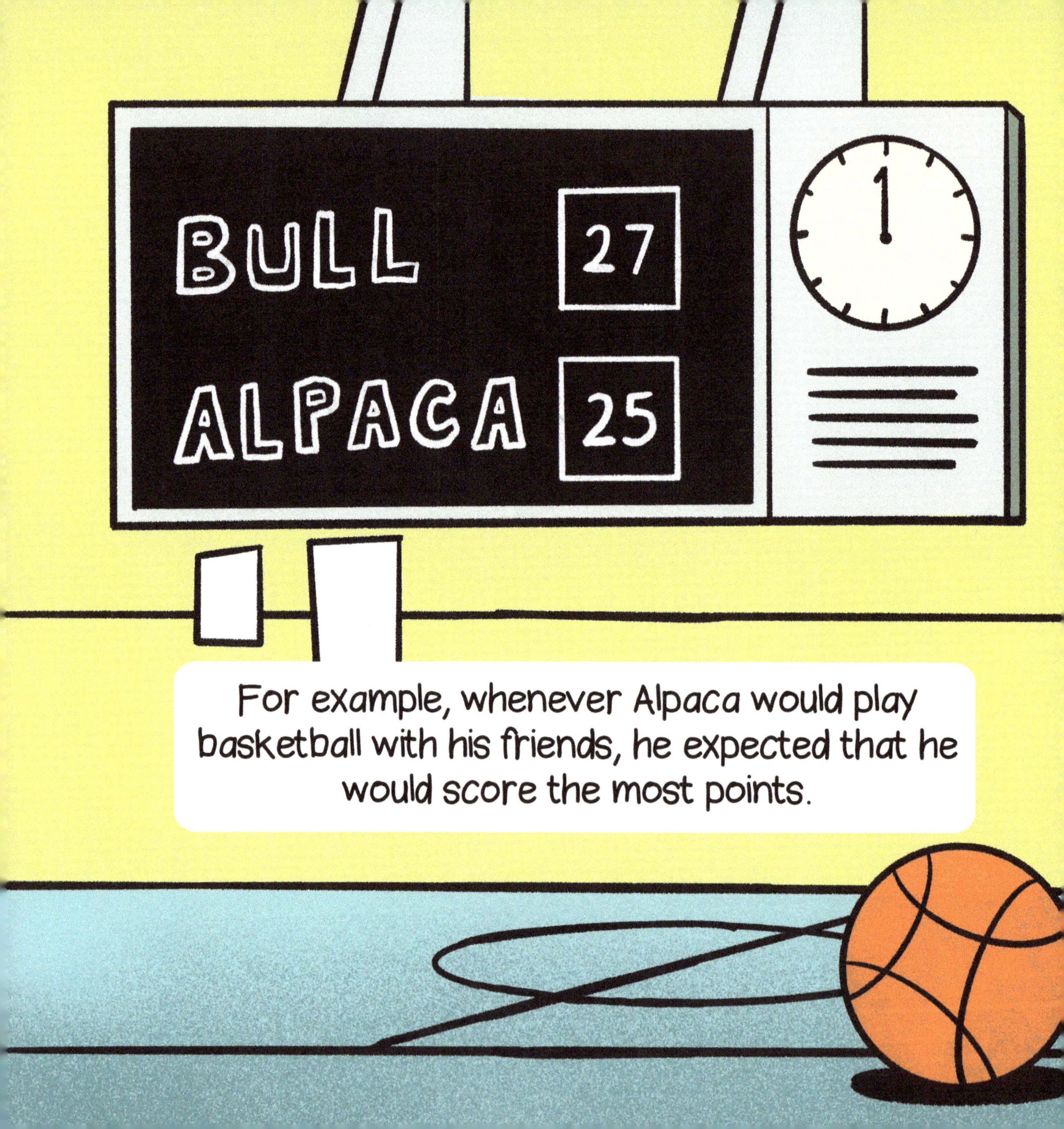

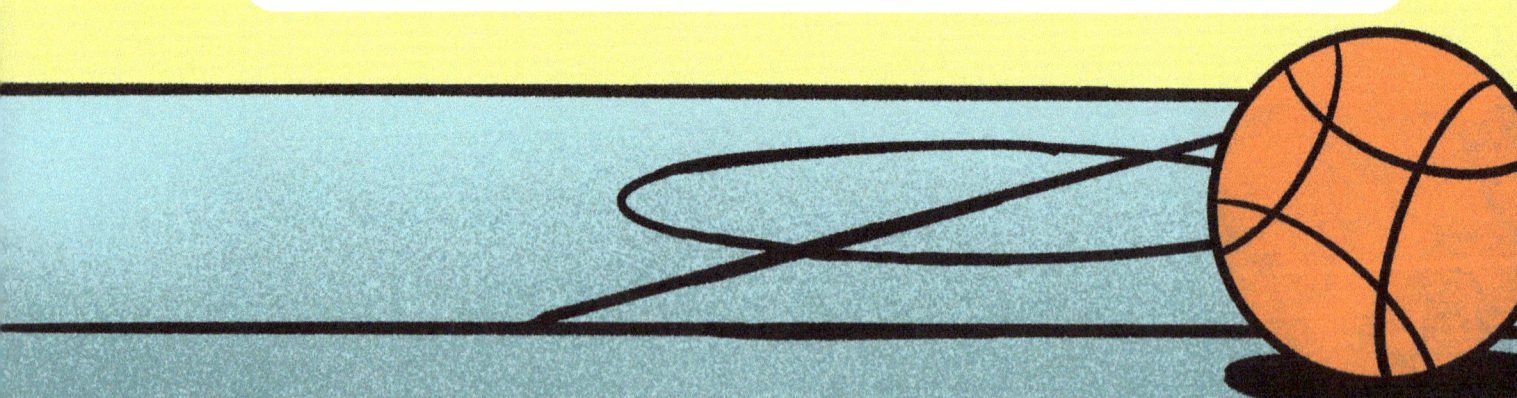

But the weather on that day was terrible, forcing the school to cancel the trip. Alpaca was so sad and cried for hours.

Fox asked Alpaca what was bothering him, and Alpaca replied, "I always want things to happen a certain way, and when they don't, I am so disappointed and anxious."

"In life, we can only control what we do, and we can only do our best. And if we do our best, that's what should make us happy."

"Use the Control Test to help you remain mentally tough, stand strong against disappointments, and control your happiness."

When Alpaca heard this, he wondered if the solution to his problems could really be this simple.

— WISHES →

— EXPECTATION →

— DESIRES →

Was it really true that he could change his expectations and control his happiness just like that?

He tried the Control Test again when he went to the park and a bunch of animals were playing on the slide. They refused to let Alpaca take a turn.

www.ingramcontent.com/pod-product-compliance
Lightning Source LLC
Chambersburg PA
CBHW042037100526